New Tools

for English Language Development

Student Book
Level 1

Santillana USA

Writers	Judie Bittinger
	Mona Scheraga
Project Director	Leland Northam
Design and Production	Real Media Solutions, LLC
Cover Art	Héctor Cuenca

The stories *No, Not Me* and *The Cow's Backyard* are adaptations of *It Wasn't Me* and *In the Cow's Backyard,* by Alma Flor Ada. ©1999, 1992 Santillana USA Publishing Co, Inc.

Parts of this book originally appeared in *Tools: English Language Development*.
published by Richmond Publishing, ©1998 by Ediciones Santillana, Inc., Guaynabo, Puerto Rico.

02 03 04 05 06   6 5 4 3 2

New Tools for English Language Development
Student Book Level 1
ISBN: 1-58105-770-9

Printed in Colombia by Panamericana Formas e Impresos S.A.

Contents

WORD BANK

1	2	3	4
book	pencil	crayon	paper

What is in your classroom?

5
scissors

6
glue

7
board

8
bookbag

Let's talk!

Let's sing!

It's Fun To Be Together
(sung to the tune of *Did You Ever See a Lassie*)

It's fun to **be** together,
Together, together.
It's fun to **be** together,
With your best friend.

sing

paint

play

read

draw

Make up more verses. **5**

Let's count!

1 one

2 two

3 three

4 four

5 five

6 six

7 seven

8 eight

9 nine

10 ten

Let's color!

1. red

2. green

3. yellow

4. blue

5. orange

6. purple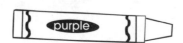

7. white

8. brown

9. black

10. pink

Let's circle and say!

1.

2.

3.

4.

5.

Let's draw and talk!

Draw your classroom.

Tell about your drawing.

Let's talk!

Let's talk about other things.

eraser / pink / table
pencil / yellow / desk
book / green / table
eraser / blue / table

What Do I See?

I come to school,
And what do I see?
I see a big classroom,
Waiting for me!

I'm in my classroom,
And what do I see?
I see my teacher,
Waiting for me!

I'm in my classroom,
And what do I see?
I see a green chair,
Waiting for me.

I'm in my classroom,
And what do I see?
I see a yellow table,
Waiting for me.

I'm in my classroom,
And what do I see?
I see white paper,
Waiting for me.

I'm in my classroom,
And what do I see?
I see a pink eraser,
Waiting for me.

I'm in my classroom,
And what do I see?
I see a purple pen,
Waiting for me.

I'm in my classroom,
And what do I see?
I see a red pencil,
Waiting for me.

I'm in my classroom,
And what do I see?
I see a blue book,
Waiting for me.

I'm in my classroom,
And what do I see?
I see new friends...
Learning with me!

MY WORD BANK

Draw your favorite words.

Tell about your drawings.

Where is it? Look, point, and say.

GO TO ALPHABET FUN.

Unit 2

I Love My Family!

WORD BANK

1	2	3	4
mother	father	brother	sister

Where are they?

5 kitchen   6 living room   7 bedroom   8 bathroom

Present a finger play!

One little house,
Closed up tight.

Open the windows
To the light.

Open the doors
For the family.

Look! Mommy, daddy,
Sister, brother, and me!

Let's draw and talk!

Draw a family member.
Tell about your drawing.

I love my _____ very much.

21

Many different families

Some families are big,
Some families are small,
Some families have three.
My family is Mommy
And me.

Different families

Now talk about your family.

Tom's family

Now talk about yourself.

This is my father.
His eyes are brown.
His hair is black.
He is tall.

This is my mother.
Her eyes are green.
Her hair is red.
She is short.

This is my grandfather.
His eyes are blue.
His hair is gray.
He is thin.

This is my baby sister.
Her eyes are blue.
Her hair is brown.
She is fat.

Now talk about your family.

The Big Turnip

One day, a grandfather planted a turnip seed.

He watered the seed. The seed grew into a plant.
The plant grew bigger and bigger.

"This turnip is ready to eat," said the grandfather.
"We can have turnip soup for dinner." So he pulled and pulled.
But the turnip did not come up.

Grandmother came to help. She pulled on the grandfather.
Grandfather pulled on the turnip. But the turnip did not come up.

Father came to help. He pulled on the grandmother.
The grandmother pulled on the grandfather. The grandfather
pulled on the turnip. But the turnip did not come up.

Mother came to help. She pulled on the father. The father
pulled on the grandmother. The grandmother pulled on the
grandfather. The grandfather pulled on the turnip.
But the turnip did not come up.

Brother came to help. He pulled on the mother. The mother pulled on the father. The father pulled on the grandmother. The grandmother pulled on the grandfather. The grandfather pulled on the turnip. But the turnip did not come up.

Sister came to help. She pulled on the brother. The brother pulled on the mother. The mother pulled on the father. The father pulled on the grandmother. The grandmother pulled on the grandfather. The grandfather pulled on the turnip. But the turnip did not come up.

Finally, the baby came to help. The baby pulled on the sister. The sister pulled on the brother.

The brother pulled on the mother. The mother pulled on the father. The father pulled on the grandmother. The grandmother pulled on the grandfather. The grandfather pulled on the turnip. And...POP! The turnip came up!

That night, the grandfather, grandmother, mother, father, sister, brother, and the baby all had turnip soup for dinner.

Let's put on a play!
Act out the story with your friends.

MY WORD BANK

Draw your favorite words.

Tell about your drawings.

I KNOW!

A. Tell about your family. Bring photos to class.

B. Make a bulletin board with all the photos.

C. Make puppets. Take turns telling "The Big Turnip" with a friend.

D. Draw a story like "The Big Turnip." Use your favorite vegetable. Tell your story.

33

GO TO ALPHABET FUN.

Unit 3

WORD BANK

1	2	3	4
skate	ride bikes	swing	play games

What are they doing?

5
read stories

6
dance

7
help

8
play music

Let's chant!

Ten good friends, dancing in a line. Alex went home for lunch.
Then there were nine.

Nine good friends, learning how to skate. Ling went home for lunch.
Then there were eight.

Eight good friends, reading about Kevin. Trang went home for lunch.
Then there were seven.

Seven good friends, picking up sticks. Charles went home for lunch.
Then there were six.

Six good friends, watching a bee hive. Bobby went home for lunch.
Then there were five.

Five good friends, playing on the floor. Nina went home for lunch.
Then there were four.

Four good friends, climbing in a tree. Carlos went home for lunch.
Then there were three.

Three good friends, making a zoo. Terry went home for lunch.
Then there were two.

Two good friends, running in the sun. Maria went home for lunch.
Then there was one.

One friend, Sally, playing all alone. She wanted to jump rope.
She wouldn't go home!

I like to. . .

I like to play softball.

I like to skate.

I like to play basketball with my brother.

I like to play tennis with my sister.

I like to play board games
with my brother.

I like to skateboard.

What do you like to do?

A busy week

Sunday

Monday

Tuesday

Wednesday

Thursday

Friday

Saturday

NOTES:

_____   _____

_____   _____

_____   _____

_____   _____

**Tell what they like to do. Start like this: Sunday.
On Sunday, he likes to skate.**

My week

Draw a pastime you like for each day.

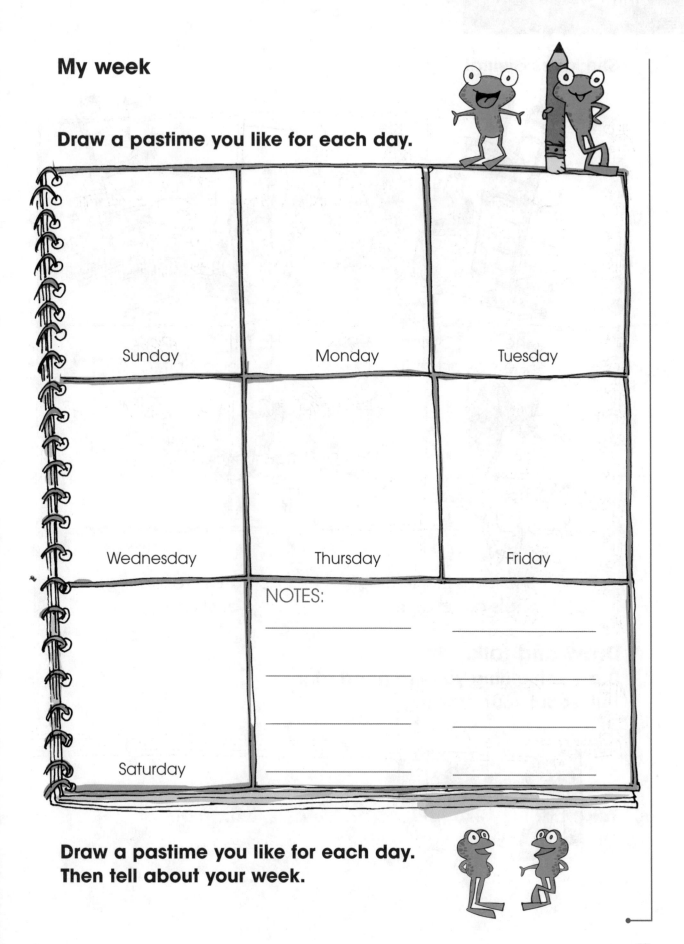

Sunday	Monday	Tuesday
Wednesday	Thursday	Friday
Saturday	NOTES:	

**Draw a pastime you like for each day.
Then tell about your week.**

She loves diving!

She loves diving.
She's good at it.

He hates diving.
He's bad at it.

She loves ice skating.
She's good at it.

He hates ice skating.
He's bad at it.

Draw and talk.
**Draw something you are good at.
Tell about your drawing.**

The Cow's Backyard

Adapted from a story by Alma Flor Ada

Illustrations by Viví Escrivá

What a wonderful day in the cow's backyard!

The ant is lying in the hammock. He's very happy.

The cow is very happy. It's a beautiful day.

And it's very nice to be with her friend the ant.

43

"Oh, look," says the ant. "There's my friend the frog."

"Croak, croak, croak," says the frog.

"Hey, frog," says the ant. "Come on. There's room
for one more friend in the hammock."

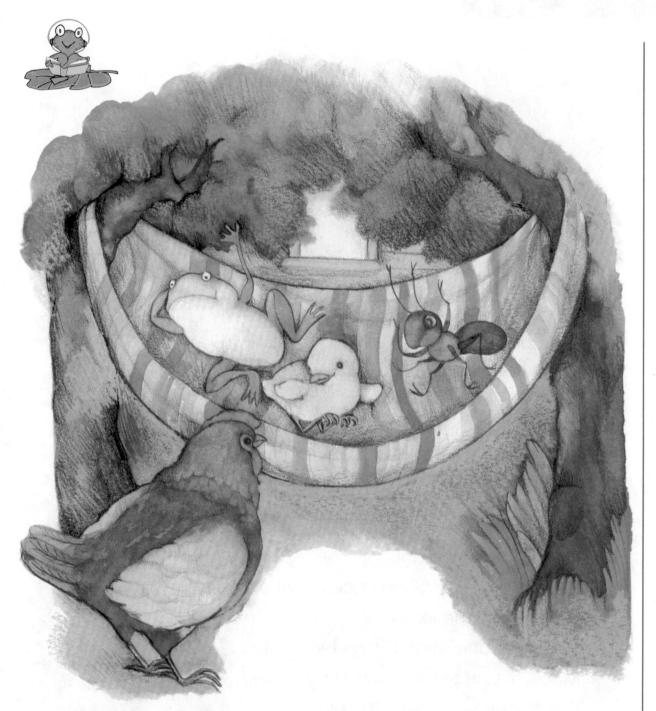

"Oh, look," says the ant. "There are my friends the hen and
the chick."

"Cluck, cluck, cluck," says the hen.

"Cheep, cheep, cheep," says the chick.

"Come on, hen. Come on, chick," says the ant. "There's room
for two more friends in the hammock."

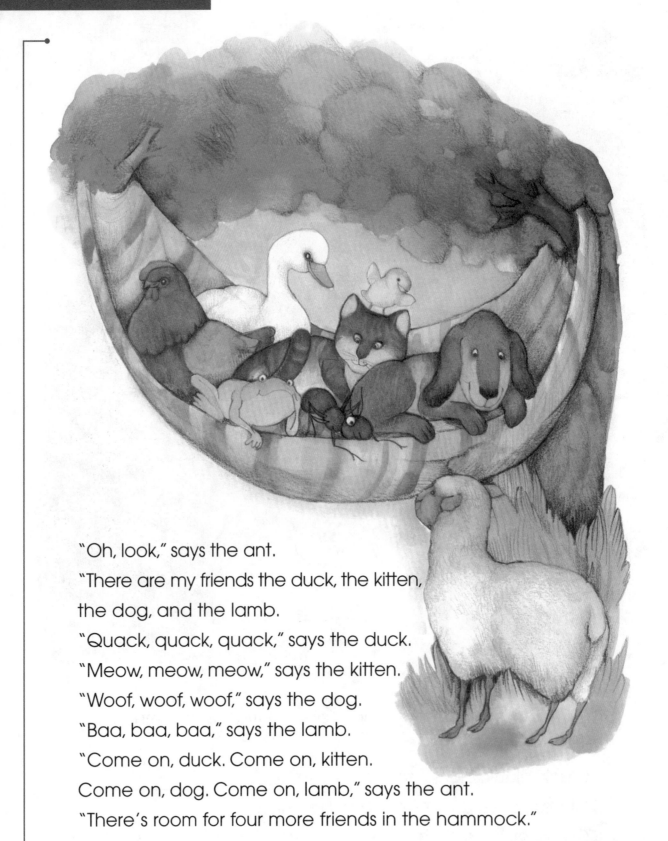

"Oh, look," says the ant.

"There are my friends the duck, the kitten, the dog, and the lamb.

"Quack, quack, quack," says the duck.

"Meow, meow, meow," says the kitten.

"Woof, woof, woof," says the dog.

"Baa, baa, baa," says the lamb.

"Come on, duck. Come on, kitten.

Come on, dog. Come on, lamb," says the ant.

"There's room for four more friends in the hammock."

"Uh-oh," says the ant. "Here comes the elephant.
There's no room in the hammock. What can we do?"
"Oh, don't worry," says the cow. "He can play with us."
"He can't be in the hammock. But he can be under
the hammock."
See? There's always room for one more friend.

MY WORD BANK

Draw your favorite words.

Tell about your drawings.

I KNOW!

PASTIMES	TONY	NATALIE
	✓	✓
		✓
	✓	✓
		✓
	✓	✓
	✓	

A. Look at the chart. Pretend you are Tony. Tell what you like to do. Begin like this: "I'm Tony. I like to skate."

B. Tell what Natalie likes to do. Begin like this: "Natalie likes to play drums."

Unit 4

WORD BANK

1	2	3	4
chicken	hamburger	bread and rolls	lemonade

50

What are they having?

5	6	7	8
cake	potato salad	jam	salad

Play food bingo!

spaghetti

corn

ice cream

tomato soup

rice

macaroni & cheese

oranges

pizza

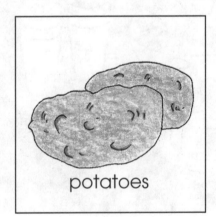

potatoes

I Love Ice Cream!

(sung to the tune of *La Cucaracha*)

I love **ice cream**,
I love **ice cream**,
Ice cream is what I like.
I love **ice cream**,
I love **ice cream**,
Ice cream morning, noon, and night!

Make up more verses.

pizza

spaghetti

tomato soup

lemonade

macaroni & cheese

What is in your favorite sandwich?

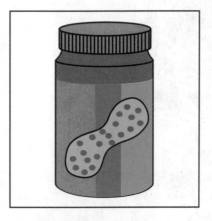

peanut butter

jelly

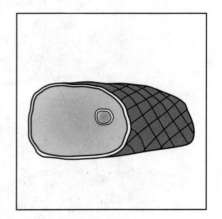

ham

cheese

tuna

lettuce

tomatoes

mustard

mayonnaise

My Favorite Sandwich

Draw your favorite sandwich.
Talk about your drawing.

Our favorites

chicken	
apples	
pizza	
spaghetti	
hamburgers	
pretzels	
cake	
ice cream	

Stone Soup

Once upon a time, a hungry soldier came to a village.

He knocked on a door.

"I'm hungry. Please give me food," said the soldier.

"We are hungry, too," said a voice from the house,

"We can't give you any food."

The solder knocked on many doors.

Each time, he heard the same thing.

"We are hungry, too. We can't give you any food."

The soldier sat down to think.

He thought up a plan.

"Bring me a big pot," he said.

"I will make stone soup for everyone."

"What is stone soup?" asked a woman.

"Bring me a big pot, and you will see," answered the soldier.

A woman brought a big pot.

"Now we need a big stone," said the soldier.

The children brought the stone.

The soldier put the stone in the pot.

And he stirred and stirred.

"Now we need some potatoes," said the soldier.

"Stone soup is better with potatoes."

A man brought some potatoes.

The soldier put the potatoes in the pot.

And he stirred and stirred.

"Now we need some carrots.
Stone soup is better with carrots."
A woman brought some carrots.
The soldier put the carrots in the pot.
And he stirred and stirred.

"Now we need some onions.
Stone soup is better with onions."
A little boy brought some onions.
The soldier put the onions in the pot.
And he stirred and stirred.

Then the soldier said he needed celery.

He said he needed beans and meat.

People brought the celery, the beans, and the meat.

The soldier put them in the pot.

And he stirred and stirred.

Finally, the stone soup was ready.

"How delicious," the village people said.

"We love stone soup."

The soldier just smiled...and ate his soup!

Draw the things that are in your favorite soup.

Write two things that are in your soup.

1._____

2. _____

MY WORD BANK

Draw your favorite words.

Tell about your drawings.

I KNOW!

A. Act out "Stone Soup."

B. Write the names of your favorite foods.

C. Buy and sell food in a grocery store.

GO TO ALPHABET FUN.

Unit 5

We Love Animals!

WORD BANK

1	2	3	4
dog	cat	turtle	snake

What pet do you have?

5	6	7	8
parrot	canary	mouse	fish

Let's sing!

Croakie Frog

Croakie Frog sings a sweet song at twilight.
She's singing as sleep comes to me.
When I wake all alone in the moonlight,
Croakie Frog sings good night from the tree.

Croakie, croakie, croakie,
Croak, croak, croak.
Croakie, croakie, croakie,
Croak, croak, croak.

Sea animals
In the ocean, you can see...

a dolphin

a seal

a whale

a penguin

an octopus

a shark

Zoo animals

At a zoo, you can see...

a lion

an alligator

a parrot

seals

zebras

Farm animals
On a farm, you can see...

pigs

chickens

horses

ducks

cows

fish

Draw and talk!
Draw your favorite animal on poster paper.
Tell about your drawing.

My Morning Walk

Adapted from a story by
Louis Carrillo and Fredrik Liljeblad

On my walk, I saw a mouse.

What did it do?

It ran away, into its little house!

On my walk, I saw a pig.

What did it do?

It said, "Oink, oink," and danced a jig!

On my walk, I saw a horse.

What did it do?

It looked in my pockets for sugar, of course.

On my walk, I saw a duck.

What did it do?

It said, "Quack, quack. Good luck!"

On my walk, I saw a cat.

What did it do?

It stretched itself, then chased a rat.

On my walk, I saw a frog.

What did it do?

It jumped and landed on a log.

On my walk, I saw a cow.
What did it do?
It said, "Moo, moo. Bye bye for now!"

How many animals did the boy see?
Which animal did he see first? Last?

Color only the animals in the story.

Time for fun

A. Make an animal mask.

B. Make egg halves. Match the halves.

MY WORD BANK

Draw your favorite words.

Tell about your drawings.

I KNOW!

Write the animal names.

_____

_____

_____

_____   _____

GO TO ALPHABET FUN.

Unit 6

Feelings!

WORD BANK

1	2	3	4
excited	**happy**	**surprised**	**sad**

How do they feel?

angry   scared   bored   tired

The Birthday Ship

The birthday ship
Is sailing, sailing
On the sea.
The birthday ship
Is bringing, bringing
Birthday gifts for me!

There are toys
In the cabins,
And toys on the decks.
And all the sailors
On the ship
Have hot dogs
Around their necks!

The Captain is a duck
With bananas on his back.
And when the ship
Gets into port,
He always says,
"Quack, quack!"

Draw and talk.

What makes you happy?
Draw a picture. Tell about your drawing.

I feel...

1. I feel happy when my mom hugs me.

2. I feel scared when my room is too dark at night.

3. I feel sad when my cat is sick.

4. I feel tired after I play soccer.

5. I feel angry when my brother takes my toys.

6. I feel bored when I watch TV.

What about you?

A Good Boy

By Robert Louis Stevenson

I woke before the morning.
I was happy all the day.
I never said an ugly word,
But smiled and stuck to play.
And now at last the sun is going
Down behind the wood.
And I am happy,
For I know I've been good.

What is the matter?

I have…

1. a sore throat.

2. a stomach ache.

3. a cold.

4. the measles.

5. a headache.

6. a cut finger.

Make up more verses.

arm

foot

knee

leg

nose

No, Not Me!

Adapted from a story by Alma Flor Ada
Illustrated by Viví Escrivá

No, it wasn't me.
No, not me!
I didn't step on the flowers.
Well, I didn't mean to.

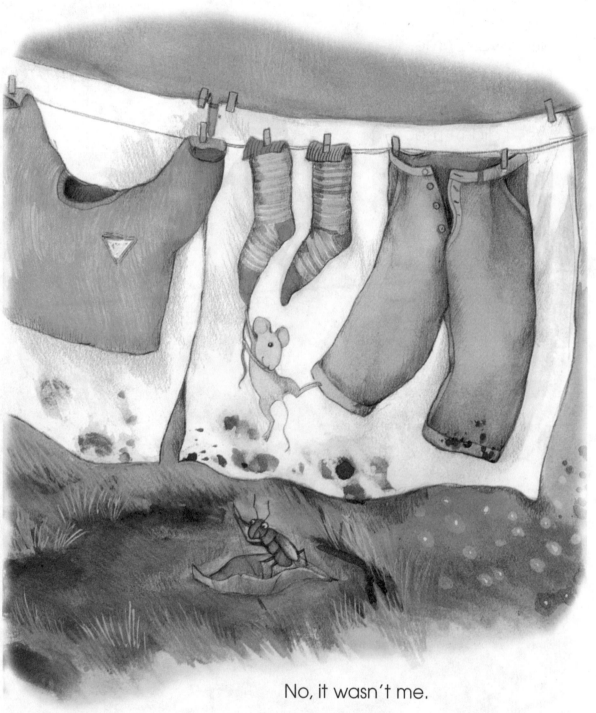

No, it wasn't me.
No, not me!
I didn't get the clothes dirty.
Well, I didn't mean to.

No, it wasn't me.

No, not me!

I didn't track mud on the porch.

Well, I didn't mean to.

No, it wasn't me.
No, not me!
I didn't spill the flour.
Well, I didn't mean to.

But, yes, it is me—
Me, me, me—
Who loves you very much!
And I'll help you clean everything up!

What happened?

What happened first? Write number 1 in the picture. What happened next? Write number 2, and so on.

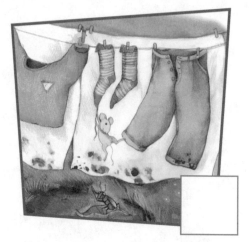

MY WORD BANK

Draw your favorite words.

Tell about your drawings.

Tell your teacher about things that make you feel like this.

1

2

3

4

5

6

97

GO TO ALPHABET FUN.

Unit 7

When I Grow Up . . . . .

1

2

5

3

WORD BANK

1	2	3	4
a pilot	a singer	a doctor	an astronaut

What do you want to be?

4

7

6

8

5   6   7   8

a
photographer

a lion
tamer

an athlete

a chef

99

Come, Look Outside the Window

(sung to the tune of *Go In and Out the Window*)

Come, look outside the window.

Come, look outside the window.

Come, look outside the window,

And tell me what you see.

I see **cars** and **buses**.

I see **cars** and **buses**.

I see **cars** and **buses**.

That is what I see!

Make up more verses.

trees and flowers

taxis and trucks

stores and houses

Draw and talk.

Draw what you see outside your window.
Tell about your drawing.

More jobs

Match the words to the pictures. Write the words on the lines.

lawyer	farmer	nurse
teacher	police officer	mechanic

1. _____ 2. _____ 3. _____

4. _____ 5. _____ 6. _____

When I grow up, I want to be . . .

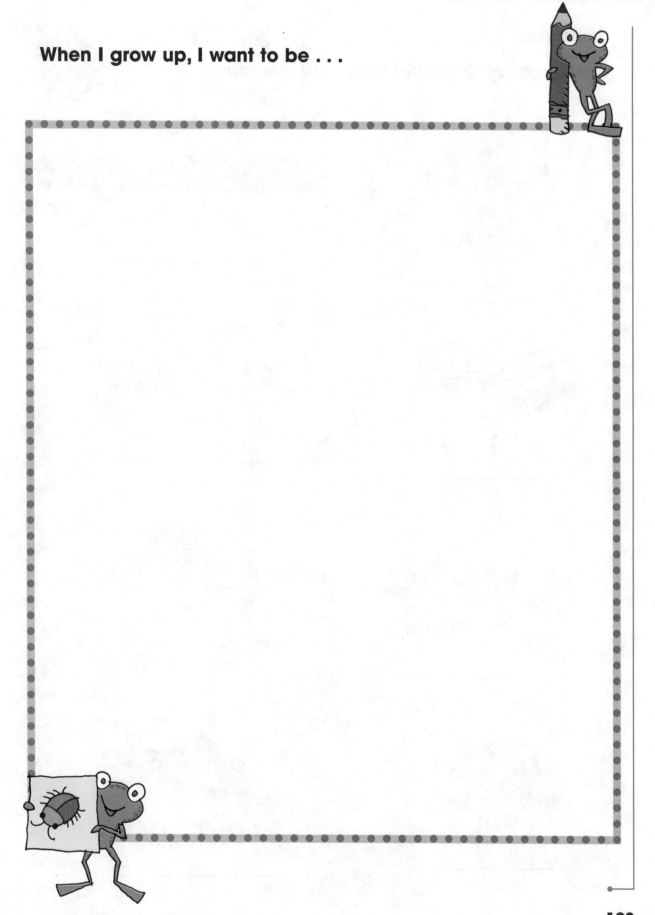

Wheels!

Copy the words on the lines. Say the words.

subway

_____

train

_____

bus

_____

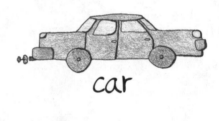

car

_____

truck

_____

taxi

_____

van

_____

motorcycle

_____

Draw and talk.

Draw a special car here.
Tell about your drawing.

When I Grow Up

What do I want to be when I grow up?

I really don't know.

I have to think about it.

Mom says I can be a nurse.
Nurses are important to a community.
But... I really don't know.

Dad says I can be an engineer.
Engineers are important to a community.
But... I really don't know.

My sister says I can be a teacher.

Teachers are important to a community.

But... I really don't know.

My brother says I can be a computer expert.

Computer experts are important to a community.

But... I really don't know.

Grandma says I can be a lawyer.

Lawyers are important to a community.

But...I really don't know.

Grandpa says I can be a farmer.

Farmers are important to a community.

But...I really don't know.

My best friend says I can be a detective.

Detectives are important to a community.

But. . . I really don't know.

I think I can be a scientist.

Scientists are important to a community.

But. . . I really don't know.

I know! A writer! I have a lot of imagination! I can write wonderful stories! I can paint pictures with words! So, now I really know. I want to be a writer when I grow up.

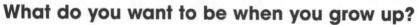

What do you want to be when you grow up?

MY WORD BANK

Draw your favorite words.

Tell about your drawings.

I KNOW!

What are their jobs? Write the words.

_____

_____

_____

_____

_____

_____

_____

_____

GO TO ALPHABET FUN.

Unit 8

Favorite Things!

1

2

3

4

WORD BANK

1	2	3	4
play computer games	draw	watch soccer	play the piano

Do you like to draw?

5 go to
the zoo

6 go to
the movies

7 go to
the park

8 go to
the beach

A Happy Little Man

I know a happy little man.
He has a happy little mouse.
They live happily together
In a happy little house.

The happy little man
Has a happy little smile.
His smile gets even bigger
When he runs a happy little mile.

They run all day on Saturday.
They run on Sunday, too.
They run and run because
They have nothing else to do!

Draw and talk.

Draw your favorite thing to do or your favorite place to go. Tell about your drawing.

When is your birthday?

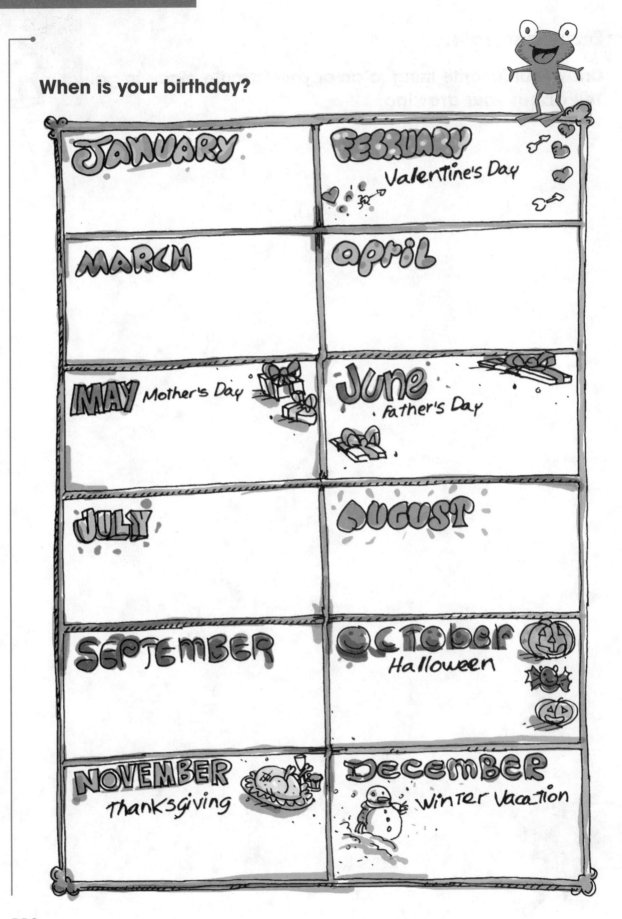

Draw and talk.

Write the name of your favorite month.
Draw what you like to do in that month.
Tell about your drawing.

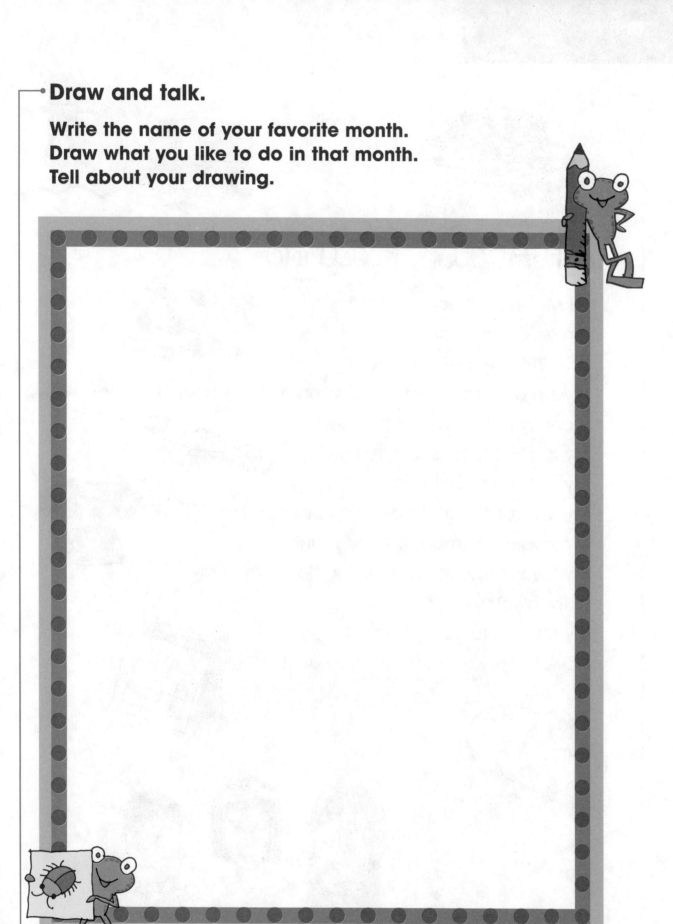

All About Rodrigo

Hi! My name is Rodrigo Santos.

I'm seven years old.

I live in Los Angeles, California.

I live in an apartment with my mom, my brother,
  and my grandmother.

My favorite food is spaghetti.

My favorite color is red.

My favorite thing to wear is my soccer shirt.

My favorite animal is the elephant.

My favorite month is February. That's when my
birthday is!

My favorite toy is my truck.

I love to play soccer. I'm good at it!

Kate's Bad Day

Adapted from a story by Lillian Mendoza

One day, Kate had a bad day at school.

She didn't want to write.

So she didn't pick up her pencil.

She didn't want to color.

So she sat on her crayons.

She didn't want to read.
So she didn't open her books.

She didn't want to eat.
So she gave away her snack.

She didn't want to share.
So she played all by herself.

Then Kate wanted to paint.
But the teacher said, "Kate, you haven't done your work today."
So Kate couldn't paint.

Kate began to cry.
The teacher said, "Don't cry, Kate. You've just been having a bad day. Tomorrow will be a better day. You'll see.
Tomorrow will be a good day."

The next day, Kate did feel better.
She wanted to write.
So she wrote a story.

She wanted to draw.
So she drew a picture for her mom.

She wanted to read.
So she opened a book and read a story.

She wanted to eat her snack.
So she ate her sandwich and drank her juice.

She wanted to share.
So she played with her friends.

The teacher said, "I'm proud of you, Kate."
You had a very good day."

The teacher gave Kate a little medal.
Kate was so happy! It really *was* a good day.

How did Kate feel at the beginning of the story?
How did Kate feel at the end of the story?
Have you ever had a bad day at school?

What is Kate doing? Look at the pictures. Write the words on the lines.

| reading | coloring | writing |
| sharing | eating |

1. Kate is _____.

2. Kate is _____.

3. Kate is _____.

4. Kate is _____.

5. Kate is _____.

MY WORD BANK

Draw your favorite words.

Tell about your drawings.

Look at the pictures. Circle the right words.

1. He likes to play
   computer games.
   the drums.

2. He likes to watch
   baseball.
   soccer.

3. She likes to play
   the piano.
   the guitar.

4. She likes to go to the
   restaurant.
   zoo.

5. She likes to go to the
   movies.
   park.

6. She likes to go to the
   beach.
   park.

129

GO TO ALPHABET FUN.

WORD BANK

1	2	3	4
mountain	ocean	desert	island

What do you see in the desert?

forest   swamp   lake   volcano

131

I Love the world!

I love the mountains.
I love the **rolling hills**.
I love the rivers.
I love the **daffodils**.
I love the sunset,
Full of bright colors.
I . . .
Love . . .
The world!

Make up more verses.

clear blue skies/butterflies

tall green trees/deep blue seas

Draw and talk.

Draw two things to take the place of the word *rivers* in the song. Talk about your drawing. Then sing your own new song!

What's the weather like?

It's a cool, rainy day.

It's a hot, sunny day.

It's a warm, cloudy day.

It's a warm, windy day.

What's your favorite kind of weather?

Puerto Rico

Puerto Rico is an island.
Where is Puerto Rico? Look at the map.
The weather in Puerto Rico is warm all year round.
Sometimes, there are hurricanes.
Puerto Rico has a beautiful rain forest.
You can see many beautiful birds there.
One beautiful bird is the Puerto Rican parrot.

DR = Dominican Republic

Let's make a parrot!

You need:
heavy paper, scissors, paint, paintbrushes, markers, a stapler, and newspaper.

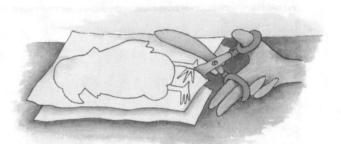

1. Put two pieces of paper together. Draw the outline of a parrot.

2. Cut both sheets of paper at the same time.

3. Paint or color both sides of the parrot.

4. Staple the two sides together. Leave a small opening.

5. Stuff the parrot with newspaper. Then staple the parrot closed.

6. Now you've got your own Puerto Rican parrot!

The Tree

Adapted from a story by Fernando Alonso

Illustrations by F. Carreño

Once upon a time, there was a tree.

It was big and strong.

But it didn't have any leaves.

The tree became sad.

It wanted to have leaves like all the other trees.

The tree talked to the sun.

"Powerful, hot sun," the tree said.

"Please give me leaves."

"I cannot give you leaves," answered the sun.

"I can only shine on the earth.

You have to find leaves for yourself."

"But I cannot," answered the tree.

"My feet are planted in the ground."

And the tree was sad.

The tree talked to the wind.

"Powerful, strong wind," the tree said.

"Please give me leaves."

"I cannot give you leaves," answered the wind.

"I can only blow on the earth.

You have to find leaves for yourself."

"But I cannot," answered the tree.

"My feet are planted in the ground."

And the tree was sad.

The tree talked to a cloud.

"Powerful, dark cloud," the tree said.

"Please give me leaves."

"I cannot give you leaves," answered the cloud.

"I can only rain on the earth.

You have to find leaves for yourself."

"But I cannot," answered the tree.

"My feet are planted in the ground."

And the tree was sad.

Children came. They saw the tree was sad.
"Let's make leaves for the tree," said the children.
"Then the tree won't be sad."

The children cut out bright pieces of paper.
They made blue leaves and green leaves.
They made yellow leaves and red leaves.

They put all the leaves on the tree.
Then they stepped back to admire the tree.

"What a beautiful tree," said the children.

"What a beautiful tree," said the sun.

"What a beautiful tree," said the wind.

"What a beautiful tree," said the cloud.

"Thank you," said the tree.

"I have beautiful leaves.

Now I'm very happy.

Thank you very much."

MY WORD BANK

Draw your favorite words.

Tell about your drawings.

I KNOW!

A. Write the places.

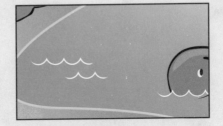

– – – – – – – – – –

– – – – – –

– – – – – – –

– – – – – – –

– – – – – –

– – – – – –

– – – – – –

– – – – – – – –

B. Write a class story.

Work with your friends. Write a story about a tree, a rainforest, an ocean—or whatever you want!

145

GO TO ALPHABET FUN.

ALPHABET FUN

Do you know all these words? Two words were NOT in this book! Which were they?

  _____

 _____

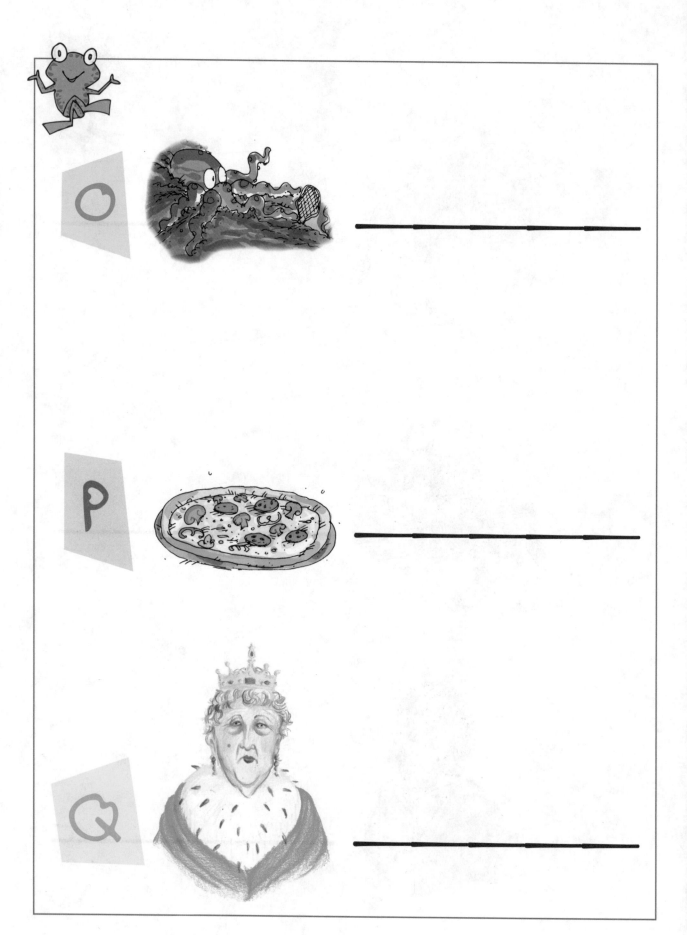

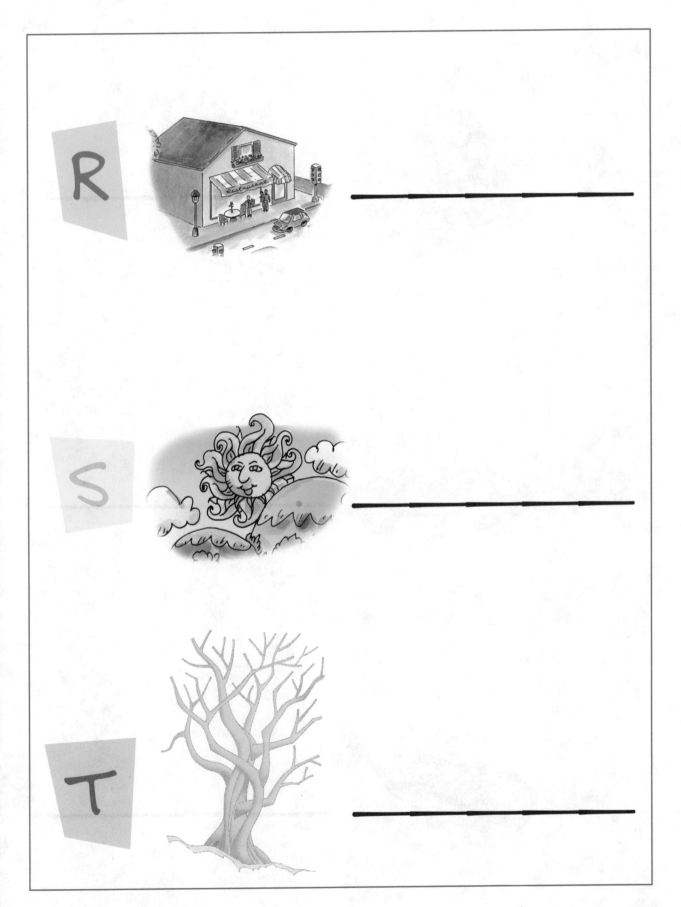

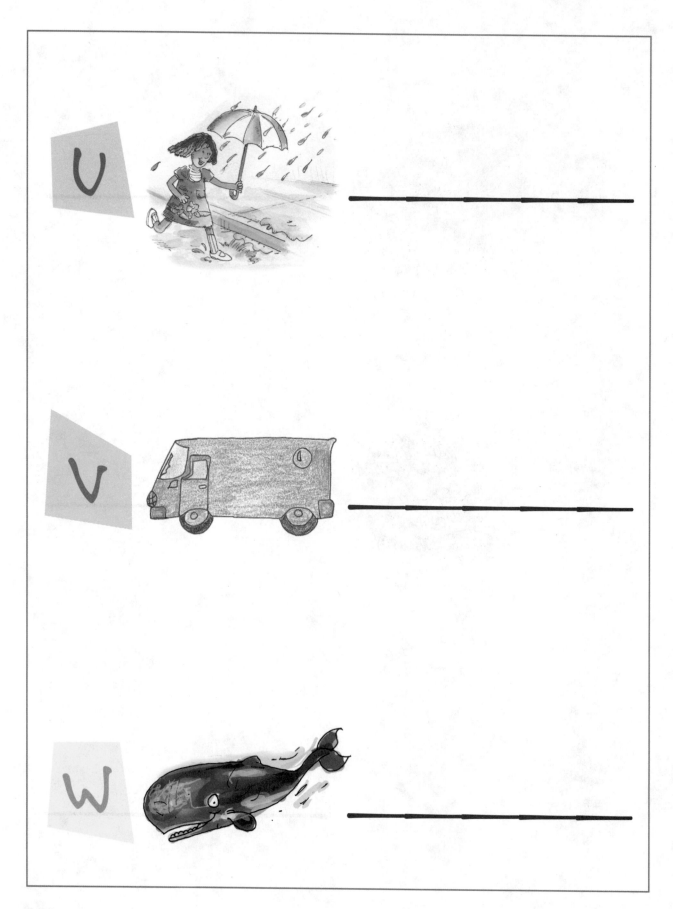

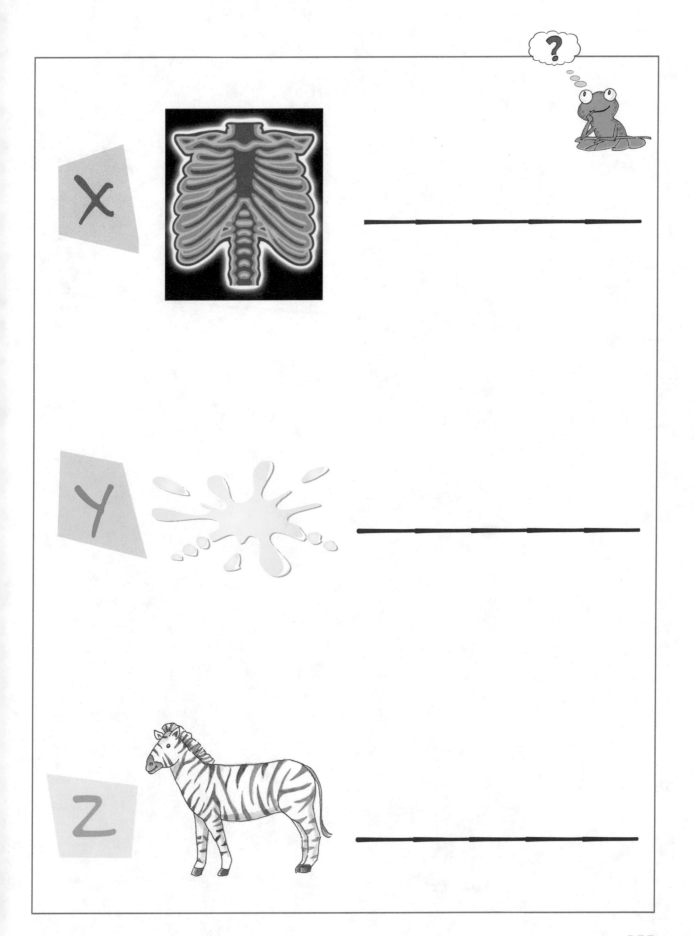